FROM SURVIVING
DIVORCE
TO THRIVING IN
SINGLENESS

5 Secrets to Wholeness While Following
Jesus and Managing a Family After Divorce

Heather Mitchell Martin

SONSET
books

heathermitchellmartin.com

From Surviving Divorce to Thriving In Singleness:
5 Secrets to Wholeness While Following Jesus and Managing a Family After Divorce
©2024 Sonset Books

First Edition

ISBN: 978-1-7371198-4-5

Published by Sonset Books and printed in the United States of America
Suggested retail price: $14.95

♥ I dedicate this book to Jesus, to Jaclyn & Jake, and to Curtis. ♥

✠

I also dedicate this book to all of the single moms who are tirelessly working each day, taking care of their kids, their home, and their jobs, shuttling kids to activities, making every meal, and stepping up financially setting the best godly example to their children. You are the stars! I promise, God has you, He has NOT forgotten you.

• • • • —————————————————— • • • •

Joel 2:25-26 "I will repay you for the years the locusts have eaten... You will have plenty to eat, until you are full, and you will praise the name of the LORD your God, who has worked wonders for you; never again will my people be shamed."

Preface

I became a Christian single mom of two children, ages six and nine, in 2010. Despite the challenges I had already faced, I was about to go through more than I thought humanly possible. I had some difficult growing to do in the areas of spiritual, financial, emotional, intellectual, and physical wholeness. But I worked hard to change my circumstances. By becoming whole in these areas, I became the best version of myself.

You might be in that place now, extended far beyond anything you could have imagined. But—GOD! Right? God gives us the strength, the resources, and the people we need to get through our most difficult times. Sometimes we are in a place where we can't, but God can. Other times, we are NOT meant to rely on ourselves because He is doing His work within us. In the midst of having to rebuild my character, my heart, my home, and my family, God showed up as He does. He put all the pieces in my path so I could become whole, and I am so grateful. The Lord put it on my heart to share these tools with other single moms.

We all work at our own pace. I worked on myself for nine years. When I started, I was in huge debt, stripped of all confidence, and my Christian friends didn't really understand what I was going through. I felt very, very alone. But—GOD.

During those years I was a single mom, the Lord shifted things in me. I learned to be healthy for myself, my children, and my future mate. If the ideas I present in this book resonate with you, great! Implement those ideas. However, some might not. That's okay too. Use what works for you but keep reading; you might find other helpful tools along the way.

A single Christian mom of young ones is a tough place to be with no support. My hope is you find you are not alone, and that you find community. Mama, you are so loved!

I promise you, "[God] is able to do immeasurably more than all we ask or imagine..." (Ephesians 3:20). I've seen it firsthand. This isn't the end. This is the beginning... of your journey to wholeness.

Ideas for Reading Through This Book

1. Begin with prayer. Ask God to help you receive all that you need to hear so that you can be healthy and whole.

2. Grab a journal and a pen.

3. Journal about the ideas in each section of each chapter.

4. Answer the questions at the end of each chapter.

FROM SURVIVING
DIVORCE
TO THRIVING IN
SINGLENESS

Table of Contents

The First Secret to Wholeness
While Following Jesus

Spiritual Wholeness

*W*here are you spiritually?

First, attending a great Bible teaching church regularly with your children is the best place to start. During this time of your life, you will need to cling to the Lord like never before. Attending church weekly greatly benefited me.

For a while, I attended two churches because I needed more of Jesus. I found a great church that had a midweek service. I needed more support, so I attended Saturday night service at one church and Sunday morning at another on weekends when I didn't have my kids.

The positive messages I heard reminded me we have a great big God who is in charge, even when it doesn't feel like it. This helped take away some of the loneliness too.

Second, serving at church is important. Find something you like to do that the kids can possibly help with, too. It could be anything from setting up, to the welcome committee, to helping in younger children's classrooms or stuffing bulletins. There are lots of things kids can help with at church.

This is a way to connect with people at church and teach your kids to give of themselves. God wants us to be giving of ourselves for His purpose with the right attitude. When we are giving of ourselves, we don't stay stuck in self-pity as long either. According to an article in the Mayo Clinic's August 1, 2023 issue, Speaking of health, "Volunteers report better physical health. Volunteering leads to lower rates of depression and anxiety.... It reduces stress and increases positive relaxed feelings."

Third, find a small group at church. This might be a mixed age/mixed gender group like a life group or a same gender group like a women's Bible study. I tried both. I know if you raise your kids full-time, it gets trickier, but do what you can.

Fortunately, many churches have online groups you can take part in, and some churches provide children's groups on adult meeting nights, too. But at a time when you feel so disconnected, it's important that you stay connected to other people who love Jesus.

Fourth, try Divorce Care. Divorce Care is a thirteen-week faith-based program that helps people hurting from a marriage break-up. Many larger churches have Divorce Care. If yours doesn't, check online for one near you.

Divorce Care makes use of videos, workbooks, and small breakout groups. There are even groups for kids to help them work through emotions that meet at the same time as the adult group.

I ended up needing to do this twice because I couldn't bring myself to do the work the first time through. I recommend showing up and soaking in all there is to offer the first time.

Fifth, find other service you can do with or without your kids. Can you volunteer once a week or once a month at a retirement home, a food bank, a homeless shelter, an animal shelter, or somewhere else? In my experience, I was able to help at a convalescent home. Most of the people were elderly. I chose this because I grew up without most of my grandparents. I served once a month when I didn't have my kids. However, when my kids came, it was a huge bonus because seniors love seeing children. Choose something that is meaningful to you.

Sixth, make time for God whether it's in the shower in the morning or lying in bed before you fall asleep. He knows how busy it is to take care of your kids on your own while working and trying to stay sane. Thank Him for what is good and all that is coming your way. Psalm 23 and Psalm 121 will get you started.

Do you have a devotional you use? If not, buy a one-page daily devotional that you can build your day around or go to sleep with at night. God will bless your time. With that, read a devotional with your kids.

When my kids were small, I would ask them to read my devotional to me on the way to school. Or you could take turns reading at the dinner table. As my children grew up, we read parts of the Bible together. Then we took some time to pray and write what we thought the verses were about separately. Fifteen minutes later, we got together to discuss. A personal adult devotional the kids and I liked is "Jesus Calling" by Sarah Young.

We never know the impact of the things we do today. When my son was in third grade, he had a project at school about family traditions. His favorite family tradition was reading devotionals on my bed with his sister and me. I didn't know it would come to be his favorite family tradition.

This might sound like a lot, or maybe you already do these things. Do what you can and add more as you can. We're called to be spiritually fit and teach our children to be like Jesus. Proverbs 22:6 says, "Train a child up in the way he should go, and when he is old, he will not depart from it."

These are ideas that helped me to stay rooted in Jesus when I felt lost. Do what helps you.

If you need to get right with Jesus to be able to walk in His love and light, do it. Whatever it takes. Lay it all at His feet. Confess sin or strongholds and walk away from them. Accept His grace and mercy so you can find freedom.

Please be encouraged, mama.

Prayer

Lord, I give you my life, the hardship and struggle, my kids, my time, my work. Lord, it is all yours. Please direct me in how to heal the hurt and pain in my own life so that I can become whole and help me to become the best parent I can for my children. You are the Great Healer. Please place your hands on my family, protect us, provide for us, heal us, and keep us close to you.

Amen

Spiritual Wholeness Questions

1. What part of spiritual wholeness is easiest for me?

2. What can I start today/this week?

3. What can be a goal for next month?

4. What can I implement in the next few months?

5. Share my plan with a close friend and ask for prayer.

The Second Secret to Wholeness
While Following Jesus

Financial Wholeness

*F*inances. Whether we have a little or a lot, God has called us to manage what He has given us. How are you handling the resources God has entrusted to you?

One epiphany I had when I became single is that I had never learned much about finances.

My parents had enough, but they never taught me to manage, make, or be a good steward of money. After I married, I worked hard and often had multiple jobs, but was always in debt. After becoming single, I decided I wanted a different way of life. I wanted financial peace.

I heard about a class at church called Financial Peace University. The cost was a hundred dollars at the time, money I did not have and did not feel like I could give up, while supporting my children by myself.

So, I prayed about it. I knew God presented this at just the right time because I had been thinking about it for several months. It was really hard to say yes, but I attended and reaped many benefits. I paid off debt, tithed, made and stuck to a budget, saved for an emergency fund, saved for vacations, and saved for retirement.

Financial Peace University by Dave Ramsey is a nine-week video course with small groups offered at church. The class teaches you how to pay off debt quickly, save money for your future, plan a budget, and so much more. I highly recommend it.

**"If it's important to you, you'll find a way.
If not, you'll find an excuse."**
— *Ryan Blair*

Another part of financial wholeness for a Christian is tithing. Because of my being in debt during my marriage, I rarely tithed (much less, tithe ten percent), but I didn't want to live that way anymore either. There are many blessings in giving back to the Lord what is rightfully His.

During my Financial Peace University class, I prayed about how and when to begin tithing. I made a deal with God, that once my debt was paid, I would tithe ten percent and save ten percent for retirement. I don't know that this is Biblically supported. I worked hard and persevered.

It took time, but by creating additional streams of income, eventually I paid off my $60,000 debt and raised my credit score. I was ready to start tithing and saving for retirement. It was about that same time a company at work came to talk about retirement plans. Again, God provided the timing.

But even more miracles happened. Shortly after I tithed regularly, a relative gave me ten thousand dollars.

Mic drop!!!

I stuck with my plan to honor God and He provided this unexpected, extraordinary, wild miracle! Never in my wildest dreams would I think someone would give me ten thousand dollars.

I can't guarantee God will always bless like that, but I continued to trust Him with my finances. As I followed the Financial Peace University plan, God helped me slowly find my way out of debt. That ALONE was a huge blessing.

Retirement is coming sooner than you think. The sooner you start saving for retirement, the better off you will be. A good financial planner can help discover what's best for you. But, regardless, you should start saving ten percent now. Or, if you're in debt like I was, drop your debt the Financial Peace University way, and then save.

Nothing is impossible.
The word itself says I'm possible.
— *Audrey Hepburn*

Another piece of financial struggle and economic hardship is how to make more money when you work full time, have kids full time, and literally have NO extra time. That's when you need to pray! God is creative and provides you gifts and talents to be used for His purpose. Tap into Him and those talents.

For instance, you may have a special ability to make money online while you sleep. I did not have that ability. When I was a teacher, I put the word out that I could tutor after school. I quickly had a few regulars. Tutoring lasted for several years with many students.

I also had housemates live with me at different times. At one point, I turned the office into my bedroom. I rented out my master bedroom with its attached bathroom. My children and I then shared the other bathroom. A different year, my living room became my friend's bedroom to help us both with finances. We moms are flexible and do whatever we can to make things work.

When my kids were not with me full time, I started a job at Starbucks (along with having housemates, tutoring, and working 7am to 4pm). But it didn't last long. Working full time with a side job plus another side hustle was too much for me.

Listen to God, listen to your body. You know when it's too much. Then rest in the Lord and listen to Him. Philippians 4:19 says, "And my God will meet all your needs according to the riches of His glory in Christ Jesus." Seek His guidance and do the footwork.

If you put some of the suggestions above to use, you can make goals regarding your finances. I have a goal sheet you can download at **https://heathermitchellmartin.com/goals-reflection-sheet** that will encourage you too. I've used something like it for many years and have been inspired and motivated by the progress I see each year.

Do keep in mind people still try to take advantage of single moms, so be careful. One of my past character defects was trusting untrustworthy people. After many years of getting my finances in order, I was swindled by a friend of seven years. I made a seventy-thousand-dollar investment and he disappeared with all of it. I was filled with shame because I did have a part in it. Looking back, I ignored many red flags. But by sharing about it, maybe I can save you from the same kind of devastation.

One of the goals I made was to take my kids on vacation—a real vacation with flights and hotels. They wanted to go to Hawaii, so I wrote it down as a goal. We had to wait until I was out of debt, but that summer we went was the year we moved to a wonderful new house near my kids' schools. I was also in the middle of my master's program. That vacation is the sweetest memory for me because I worked so hard to make it happen, and we had the BEST time. I believe we have a God who is with us and for us as long as we move forward in accordance with His will.

That summer we moved to a new house was another testimony to the Lord.

The house we were supposed to move into fell through. I wrote a letter to the owner of another house, explaining I was a teacher in the school district, and we had been trying to move to live within walking distance of my children's schools. I sent a picture of us, and we prayed.

So, what did God do?

One of the ways I served at church was volunteering at the newcomers' luncheons each quarter. I checked in names and welcomed people.

A gentleman approached me at the luncheon that Sunday. He stated his first and last name. In shock, I repeated his name while checking him off the list, then added, "Who lives on Cayente Street."

He was confused, but God was working. I introduced myself and explained how I wrote him a letter about moving into his home. I told him how beautiful it was and walked him to his seat, where I introduced him to a few more people. I didn't make it awkward, but I believe it was a divine appointment.

After seating him, I went back to my post checking in other newcomers.

This was in May. We closed escrow on that house a week after school got out for the summer. A week later, we left for Hawaii.

I don't know your dreams or goals for yourself or your family. But God makes dreams come true. If it has not happened for you yet, just wait. Wait for the miracle; He is always working on our behalf.

Prayer

Lord, thank you for how you've provided for me thus far. Today, I surrender my finances to you and ask that you would make me teachable. I pray for guidance in creative ways to change my financial situation and I pray that you would bring positive change to my finances so that I can experience financial freedom and give back to you in extraordinary ways. I know you are in charge, Lord. Thank you for bringing me hope.

Amen

Financial Wholeness Questions

1. What is my biggest financial struggle?

2. Where do I need to start financially?

3. What will be my financial goals in the next month? 3 months? How will I achieve them? Write my goals here.

_____

_____

_____

_____

_____

_____

_____

_____

_____

_____

_____

_____

_____

_____

The Third Secret to Wholeness
While Following Jesus

Emotional Wholeness

> **I am not what happened to me,**
> **I am what I choose to become.**
> — *Carl Gustav Jung*

*I*n this time of life there is a lot we can do to take care of ourselves. Yes, you heard me. It's time we take care of ourselves!

We spend much of our time taking care of children, husbands, family members, friends, and people at church. We often forgot about ourselves.

I've had years when the only clothes I bought were from Costco because I couldn't shop anywhere for myself. You can probably relate. I don't believe the Lord wants us to forget ourselves and become so depleted we have nothing of ourselves left to give. In Matthew 22:39, Jesus reminds us, "...Love your neighbor as yourself." He doesn't say love your neighbor instead of yourself. So, during this difficult time of life, be gentle and think about how you can take care of yourself better. We CAN place value on what WE need and feel.

Emotional wholeness could take a lifetime to achieve, but every step you take to better care for yourself will help. You are the example to your children of what healthy looks like. Children don't see what you say as much as what you do; they pay attention to your actions. So, practice what you preach.

There is so much brokenness in the world. If you came from dysfunction like I did, you may have married someone as unhealthy as you, or worse.

But there is hope in Jesus! He gave us many tools here on earth to help heal our hearts and our lives. Once we are healthy, we attract healthier people into our lives.

In an earlier chapter, I talked about a beautiful Bible-based program called Divorce Care, which I think is the first step toward emotional wellness during and after divorce. But there are so many other wonderful tools.

For many of us, individual therapy is needed. You may be wrestling with God about the loss of your marriage, the loss of dreams, the loss of family, or you may have been in an abusive relationship, or were dealing with a partner with mental illness or addictions. You may need professional help.

If you choose this path, please find a Christian therapist who points you to Jesus while you heal. One of my therapists introduced me to a book called, "The Grief Recovery Handbook." It helped me work through the grief I felt from my marriage ending and addressed other past traumas and people that caused great grief in my life.

The book contains many questions to answer. Much of it you can read and do on your own, but it is designed for you to meet with a therapist after doing the work. Author Melody Beattie says, "Sometimes we begin to believe grief, or pain, is a permanent condition. Feeling our feelings, instead of denying or minimizing them, is how we heal from our past and move forward into a better future."

Many of us don't even know HOW we feel at any given time. I was used to basic emotions like happy, sad, and mad. A feelings wheel helped me a lot.

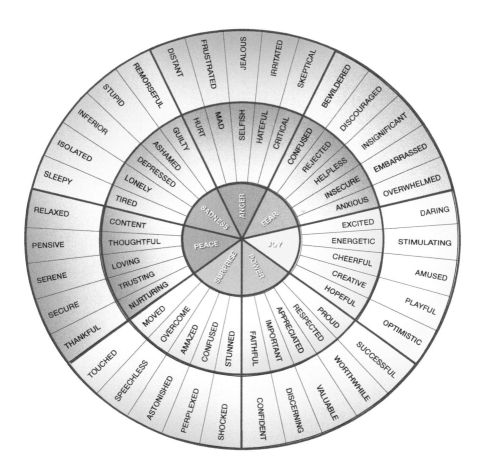

One year, I practiced a technique in the morning using the book, "Make Miracles in Forty Days." It was very therapeutic. I often went from enraged and frustrated, to crying because I felt hurt and disappointed. Then, by the end of the short exercise, my emotions changed to grateful and serene. I learned how to use all of my emotions and apply many of them in a short period of time, using just a few minutes every morning. I went through so many emotions so quickly, I felt lighter throughout each day. I was able to email these to a friend who never responded... just let me send them. What a gift those days were.

If you are depressed you are living in the past.
If you are anxious you are living in the future.
If you are at peace you are living in the present.
— *Lao Tzu*

I was introduced to an incredible program called Al-Anon in 2009. Al-Anon is a support group for families and friends of alcoholics and addicts. Although the common denominator is people who have an alcoholic or addict in their life, the ideas and readings provided by these groups help better relationships overall by teaching you how to deal with very difficult people or someone else's mental illness. If you are a caretaker who cares "too much," you may need Al-Anon to help you recover from codependency.

I have met many good friends in Al-Anon, but one story I need to share is how God used my ex-husband to bring a best friend into my life.

One night, I met a woman at Al-Anon who recognized my children because she had seen them at church, where she served with my ex-husband. She had been on a few dates with my ex.

The next time we met at a meeting, she told me she had called off any more dates. She knew why God had her meet him... it was so she and I could become great friends.

We are still very close. We even lived together before she remarried.

There are Al-Anon meetings all over the world every day of the week, many times during the day. There are many meetings online as well. Visit Al-Anon.org to find a meeting in your city.

It is suggested you try six different meetings before deciding if Al-Anon is right for you. It feels like therapy to me, but costs nothing (a one-to-two-dollar donation). I get to learn through and from others daily. Although we say 'Higher Power' in meetings, many people talk about God. It is a place where people come together from all walks of life, not just Christians.

If you feel more comfortable with other Christians, many churches have something similar called Celebrate Recovery. I attended Celebrate Recovery for several years, but Al-Anon's tools of recovery changed my life, and I continue to go today. I had to rewire my thinking and how I responded to situations (people, places, and things) so I could lead a healthier way of life for me and my children.

When I first heard I should be taking care of myself, I had no idea what that meant. Later in my journey, I was encouraged to make a list of things that make me feel good (and are good for me). This took some time because I didn't know myself well enough to know what made me feel good. I had lost myself in making sure everyone else was okay. I forgot about myself.

Take time over the next week (or weeks) to think about what makes you happy, peaceful, or calm. Make a list of things that nurture your soul. Here are a few ideas on my list: hiking, going for walks, sitting at the beach, baths with candles and Epsom salts, listening to music, praying, calling a friend, reading, and doing something artsy. When I was a little more in my prime, kickboxing and Zumba were on that list too.

Make sure the things on your list help change your mood positively.

I also really enjoy book clubs and self-help books. I wasn't taught healthy ways in my family of origin, so I learn a lot by reading. There is a list of suggested reading at the end of this book that greatly changed my perspective, encouraged my soul, and helped my emotional wellness.

The best and most beautiful things in the world
cannot be seen or even touched.
They must be felt with the heart.
— *Helen Keller*

Boundaries. Have you heard of boundaries? How are you doing with them? Are you able to say yes and no when you mean it, or do you end up doing things you don't want to do to please others? Setting clear boundaries is part of self-care. I highly recommend the book "Boundaries" by Henry Cloud. He is a Christian author that explains in detail the problems with not having boundaries and how to implement them. Be aware: if you haven't had boundaries before now, the people in your life may not like this change. There will be push back, but you need to continue setting boundaries because they are good for you and those around you.

God gave Adam and Eve boundaries. He established them to protect freedom and intimacy in the garden, but when violated, the Lord delivered consequences that we still feel today.

Boundaries help us feel safe in relationships. However, sometimes by the time we realize we need boundaries, it's not a small change. We've allowed people to walk all over us for a long time and we need a life overhaul in the boundary department.

Other outstanding books on this topic include "Boundaries with Kids" by Henry Cloud, "Boundaries with Teens" by John Townsend, "Good Boundaries and Goodbyes" by Lysa Terkeurst, and "Boundaries in Dating" by Cloud and Townsend.

When was the last time you had fun? Part of your emotional wholeness includes having fun and enjoying life. You may need a night out, a weekend away, or a vacation with the kids. All of these are possible with or without the funds... but it takes praying and imagination.

Sometimes watching someone else's kids for a while will give you some much needed down time when their parents reciprocate. Maybe someone you know owns a cabin, or you could swap houses with someone that lives a little farther away. Can you go camping with friends or on your own?

It's funny, but sometimes when life gets really tough, that's when our creativity goes into high gear. One summer, I wanted to take the kids on vacation, but I was broke. I had a friend whose family had a Timeshare and was willing to let us rent it. It was cheap because it was at the worst time of the year to go to the desert. The days were 118 degrees, but it had several pools, a kid's club with all kinds of activities, and entertainment for all of us to do at night.

Two weeks before the trip, I had a meltdown. The place had a kitchen, so we were going to bring our own food, but I didn't have the money to buy any. My friend walked me over to my freezer and said to eat everything in the freezer... and to use our canned food in the pantry.

I didn't love the idea, but I didn't have any other options. So, I made a list of food items and paired them together. I soon realized a theme came to my mind with each dinner. I wrote down themes like Italian, Red Carpet, Under the Sea, Hawaiian, French, Prehistoric night, etc. During the vacation, the children created backdrops and scenery for each theme, so it was a built-in craft time every day.

For example, along with spaghetti and bread on Italian night, the kids made paper placemats of the Leaning Tower of Pisa and we used red, white and green crepe paper to decorate. We dressed up in fancy outfits and walked down the handmade red carpet for Red Carpet night, had soup and fishy crackers when we went Under the Sea with The Little Mermaid movie, ate French toast and watched Ratatouille during French night, and made colorful flowers out of tissue paper to enhance our teriyaki and pineapple Hawaiian meal. I could go on, but you get the idea.

Bottom line, it was a great vacation because we didn't buy anything new. We just brought what we had around our houses to create fun theme nights the kids looked forward to each day.

Another way to heal emotionally is to tap into your creativity. Make time to create art, practice music or learn a new instrument, dance in a class or on your own, write fun or heartfelt poetry, journal, or write stories. Using the arts in your life can be cathartic and help release emotions and feelings that need to pour out somewhere.

I liked lettering and collages, so I turned part of my closet into a craft area where I could make greeting cards with colored papers, photos, stickers, and stamps. This outlet made my heart happy. I still need a creative outlet.

At one point, my children and I all took guitar lessons. On another occasion, I took drum lessons. My daughter and I were even in a show where we played a duet—she was on guitar and I was on the drums. These days

there are all kinds of music lessons on YouTube. If that was an option back in the day, we would have taken guitar or ukulele lessons online.

I have been journaling for many years. It was actually a cross between journals and my prayers to God. For a few years, I turned parts of my journal time into an artsy meditation on whatever I was reading in the Bible. I also create a dream board in January every year after I fill out my goals and reflection sheet (**heathermitchellmartin.com/goals-reflection-sheet**).

I cut pictures out of magazines that help me focus on what I want out of the next year.

Recently, I have seen many churches and cities provide support groups for single moms. Look for these resources online or ask your church. There was nothing like this when I was going through my divorce, but I'm so grateful for these new resources. You don't have to be alone in this.

I know how lonely it feels and how isolating it can be. I definitely felt like the only Christian going through divorce at my church—or in my town. If you have a choice, even if it's hard, try to be part of something where the people around you are going through what you are. There is healing in community.

A lot of us feel mom guilt as well. As a single mom, we have even more mom guilt. But no single mom has all the finances and resources to do everything she wants with her kids. I would say most parents, even when there are two, can't give their children everything they want to give them.

We are not perfect. But if you are teaching your children how to be the best version of themselves by taking care of yourself, loving others, and following the Lord, you will do an amazing job raising your little people.

Psalm 23:4 Even though I walk through the darkest valley, I will fear no evil, for you are with me; your rod and your staff, they comfort me.

Prayer

Lord Jesus, in Proverbs 4:23 it says, "Above all else, guard your heart, for everything you do flows from it." It is so true. I thank you for the tools you have given me to take care of my emotional health. Please help me make my emotional health a priority so I can be the example my children need. You give me your word, prayer, therapy, small groups, and so many other tools to change my inner beliefs about myself and to make me whole again. I believe I was made in Your image. I believe what You say I am… I am God's child (John 1:12), I am a friend of Jesus (John 15:15), I have been chosen by God and adopted as His child (Ephesians 1:3-8), I have been redeemed and forgiven of all my sins (Colossians 1:13-14), I am God's workmanship (Ephesians 2:10), I have not been given a spirit of fear but of power, love and a sound mind (2 Timothy 1:7). Thank you for your truths, Jesus. I believe them.

Amen

1. What small thing can I do TODAY for my emotional health?

2. List 6-10 things that make me feel good (and are good for me) that I can put into practice regularly to take care of myself or I can use as a pick-me-up.

3. What can I start doing this month for my emotional health?

4. What are my emotional health goals for this year?

The Fourth Secret to Wholeness
While Following Jesus

Intellectual Wholeness

ntellectual Wholeness increases your self-esteem, which contributes to your emotional health as well. Thinking long term, you must decide how to best care for yourself and your children.

This may require more schooling or vocational training. You may need to make decisions about how to take care of your family. Or you may need to find some short-term jobs. Whatever you need to do, pray about it first. Ask the Lord to guide you and use the gifts and talents He's given you to bless your family and further His kingdom.

I had wanted to get my master's degree since I was first married. Thirteen years later, I still hadn't gone back to school. But my story wasn't over, and neither is yours.

One day, God started opening doors after praying about it for many years. I found a master's program that used the arts (I was an elementary school teacher) that took place on weekends. The program required more prayer, talking to my ex, and $12,000 I didn't have. But when God is in control, there is no stopping His plans.

I started talking about going back to school with friends. Soon after, a Christian friend in Al-Anon told me about a women's group that provided scholarships and loans for Christian women choosing to obtain a higher degree. After she recommended me, I filled out the application and was interviewed by a panel. I received a $1,200 scholarship. I also received a loan for the rest of school. There was one condition—I needed a co-signer. Why? Because even though I worked full time and owned a home, I hadn't paid off my enormous debts yet.

Thankfully, even though I was nearing forty, my parents co-signed for me. My ex-husband also agreed to the new change in schedule and my prayers became prayers of gratitude.

Your story will differ from mine, but keep in mind we have a big, HUGE God who loves you dearly and wants good things for you and your family.

As I look back on life, I continue to see how God showed up and worked miracles in my life. You have the same God I do. Psalm 37:4 tells us, "Delight yourself in the Lord, and He will give you the desires of your heart." This verse means that when you want what Jesus wants, when you're aligned with Him, your desires are His desires.

You're braver than you believe, stronger than you seem, and smarter than you think.

— *Winnie the Pooh*

If you don't know where to begin, start with prayer. After praying about direction, take a free personality test (such as the Jung Typology Test) to learn your Briggs Meyers personality type. (**https://www.human metrics.com/tests**) The results may help explain your personality and offer a list of career paths your personality type might be better at, resulting in increased enjoyment.

Other ways to help find a new career might be to listen to motivational speakers, or take business, real estate, cosmetology, or yoga classes online or at a junior college near you. You might even consider meeting with a career coach. Whatever you do, don't let any challenge stop you; don't let what someone else says about you stop you from changing your life. You are smart, gifted, capable, and the daughter of the KING.

Prayer

God, thank you for how much you have provided so far. Lord, I know you want me to be able to take care of my family. Please help me use the gifts and talents you've given me for your kingdom, direct me to find a job / career that will provide well for my family. Thank you for directing my next steps. I will look for where You are leading me. You are Almighty.

Amen

Intellectual Wholeness Questions

1. Do I struggle in this area? What do I want or need to change?

2. What is my first step to make a change?

3. What are my goals in this area for this year? For the next 2 years? In the next 3-5 years? 6-10 years from now?

_____

_____

_____

_____

_____

_____

_____

_____

_____

_____

_____

_____

_____

The Fifth Secret to Wholeness
While Following Jesus

Physical Wholeness

Exercise reduces feelings of depression and stress, and it enhances mood and overall emotional well-being. So, it's time to get active for your emotional and physical health. Again, your children are watching. What you value, they will value.

If you have kids full time, you can go on walks around the neighborhood while they ride bikes, lift handheld weights at home, walk (in your living room) with Leslie Sansone or do Yoga with Adriene (my favorite yoga) on YouTube.

When it came to exercise and spending time with my son, I had to think outside the box. There are some 'boy' things that didn't come naturally for me, even though I played a lot of sports growing up. I realized I needed to take my son fishing, go to the batting cages, and learn to hit golf balls at the driving range.

Once I started talking about it, grown kids or husbands of friends taught me how to prepare for these things. One friend even put together a small tackle box for the first time I took my son fishing.

Just so you know, even though I had prepared, God provided even more. On our first fishing trip, I brought the fishing pole, scissors, line, tackle box... everything I had researched. But when we got to the fishing spot, a friend's older son was unexpectedly there with a buddy. They were using hot dogs as bait (I never thought to bring hot dogs to catch fish). Thankfully, they shared their knowledge and supplies. God just kept showing up.

I find boys need a type of physical contact that girls don't require. Early on, I bought my son a punching bag. When he got angry or frustrated, he went to the garage and punched that bag. I think it helped our family of three. As the kids hit middle school, they could join me at the gym. My son enjoyed a boxing ring, treadmill, and bike until he got old enough for weights. My daughter took classes and used the treadmill or bike.

Personally, I've also enjoyed a lot of yoga over the years. The calmness that came with it did a world of good for me. Not only did it make me stronger, but I slowed down; I paid attention to the small, simple things. I quieted my heart and mind. Some days, moms need this to find sanity.

That's not all I did, either. I had a gym membership during my marriage that I kept after I divorced. Going to the gym with a few friends helped in more ways than one to reduce the tension in my life. I also attended Zumba, went to kickboxing and yoga classes, learned to use weights, played racquetball, and sat in the sauna.

If none of that interests you, there are plenty of other activities to choose from. Attend a hula class, a sailing class, or a dance class; learn to surf, paddleboard, or play tennis; buy a jump rope; or do cross-country skiing or water aerobics. No matter what, get moving so those happy endorphins can be released and do their job and help you feel better!

Maybe you like hiking, like I do. I always hiked my local hills with a friend to be safe.

However, one time I went hiking alone. I would love to say I was wrestling with God, like Jacob. But it probably wasn't quite as godly as Jacob's wrestling. I prayed while I hiked, and I got angry at the Lord about how my life was turning out. While telling God how upset I was, I fell.

I slid down the hill for ten feet on my knees. When I finally stopped, my knees were bloody, I was covered in dirt, and there wasn't a soul in earshot. It took time to recover and stand again. I left that day limping. I felt like when I got upset, He let me know, "But Heather, I am still in control." I can't imagine doing this life without God. I will not leave Him.

Even now, many years later, I am reminded of that day by the scar on my knee. Jesus loves me and will not leave me. Maybe that was the beginning of my blessing. Maybe it took a breaking point to get real with the Lord. It's hard when things don't make sense in life, but so often we cannot see what the Lord is doing. He turns the worst of us and the most awful circumstances into something beautiful. We just need to trust our Maker and His timing.

A friend of mine once described how our life with the Lord is like rock climbing. God is the belayer (the one holding the safety rope). As we climb our way through life, we may go to the left or to the right, choosing different grips than someone else. But if we go too far left or too far right, God pulls the rope tight to gently direct us back on track. We all take a different path, but we still get there, and He is always ready to catch us.

> **Take care of your body.**
> **It's the only place you have to live.**
> — *Jim Rohn*

Remember, exercise is just one way to help you feel more balanced and get to a healthier place! Our body is God's temple. Let's take care of it.

Healthy eating is another way to honor what God has given us. We need plenty of nutrients to keep our bodies strong. To accomplish that, we need to eat healthy, whole foods without too many sweets and carbohydrates.

When we eat too many sugars, we only crave foods that cause headaches, inflammation, heart disease, depression, weight gain, and high blood pressure. The more lean meats, veggies, and fruits we eat, the better we feel. If this is an area of difficulty in your life, Lysa Terkeurst wrote a brilliant book called "Made to Crave" that could help you on your journey.

Visiting the doctor is yet another way to take care of your physical well-being. Go to your primary doctor, your OB/GYN, the dentist, the optometrist, and the chiropractor often. Make appointments for whatever services you need and have access to. Again, your children watch your example.

It was early in my divorce that I became very ill. My hair fell out in heaps, my body was extremely cold, I had brain fog, I was extra sleepy, I gained weight, and I was depressed. My doctor wanted me to stay home from work for two weeks and start antidepressants. Although I had used antidepressants in the past, I didn't believe that was the reason for all these symptoms. It didn't add up. I asked her to keep looking.

The doctor took blood tests and found out I had an autoimmune disease. So, I modified my diet and added vitamins and another medication. Soon, I witnessed changes to my body's functioning. But I still needed help. I needed medical professionals to walk with me.

Wherever you are in your health journey, I encourage you to take some positive steps in the right direction. For you. For your children.

Prayer

Lord Jesus thank you for the beautiful, strong body you've given me. I pray that I will honor your temple by decreasing the stress in my life through exercise and healthy eating. Let me get active, help me to release the feelings and emotions I have so that I can have happy endorphins fill my body. Thank you for wonderful doctors who can help me live my best life. I pray for the time, the means, and the willingness to add these healthy benefits to my life.

Amen

Physical Wholeness Questions

1. What exercise is already part of my life?

2. What type of exercise(s) would I like to add to my life to help reduce the emotional burden?

3. How will I make this happen?

4. What do I need to change with my eating habits?

5. What doctor appointments do I need to make?

6. Share these things with a trusted friend.

_____

_____

_____

_____

_____

_____

_____

_____

_____

_____

The Secret's Out...

*H*ealing is painful. But it's time.

It's time to make positive, lasting changes. It's time to forgive yourself for the bad choices you've made. It's time to forgive others so you can live happy, joyous, and free. It's time to embrace being human. It's time to make choices that are good for you.

Brave is a decision you get to make as you face reality and heal. Jesus said it clearly to a person who requested healing in John 5:8: "Do you want to be made well? Then pick up your mat and walk."

You have the tools. The Lord is present to help you. It is time.

Have you heard of Kintsugi? Kintsugi is a Japanese art that involves putting broken pottery pieces back together with gold. God does this with us as we face our pain and heal. By embracing the flaws and imperfections

in our lives, with His guidance, we can create an even stronger, more beautiful life.

God can use the things in this world that wreck us the most. He brings beauty from ashes. He takes broken pottery and creates something new and more treasured than even before.

He is the Healer, the Restorer, the Miracle Worker. We can trust Him. Mama, YOU are the daughter of the most high King. That means you are safe, secure, loved, wanted, good enough, and have purpose. Read that again. Own it. Write it down for yourself and infuse it into your being.

You may be going through trials of many kinds but put your hope in Him and know that your story ISN'T over. In Mark 5:34, Jesus told a woman dealing with severe pain, "Daughter, your faith has healed you. Go in peace and be freed from your suffering." Our faith heals us.

Surrendering to the Lord has wonderful consequences. I've discovered that what is on the other side is extraordinary. Embrace the messiness of being human and trust the God of the Universe.

You may remember the hymn, "I Surrender All."

All to Jesus, I surrender.
All to Him, I freely give.
I will ever love and trust Him,
In His presence daily live.

Live this hymn. Live in obedience to Him and He will be with you and bless you. Life is forever changing. Be open to what that looks like as you trust your Lord and Savior for this next season.

Right now, if you have children, your purpose is to raise good humans who love and follow Jesus. You will see all you've poured into them; the unending hours of sweat and tears, all of it counted.

By healing and becoming whole yourself, you are changing the trajectory of your children's lives and their children's lives. You are making lasting changes that will leave a family legacy of healthier, godly living for generations to come.

You've got this Mama!

Xo
Heather

Writing this book began because the Lord put it on my heart to share how I made it through my single mom life. When I became single, I had a lot of growing to do. I worked hard for many years to become emotionally healthy, learning to rely more and more on Jesus. I also knew I wanted to be physically and intellectually strong, so I sought to improve in those areas. I struggled financially and wanted to change my relationship with money as well.

During my time as a single mom, I was stretched and challenged like never before in my life. But during that difficult time, I was going through a metamorphosis. The struggle was needed so I could become strong in Christ—just like the caterpillar takes time to grow and change before becoming a beautiful butterfly. God challenged me in such a way that I depended totally on Him and not on the people or things of this world.

I am no longer a single mom, but for nine years, I was the sole provider and emotional support for my kids. With God I learned how to be the best version of myself so I could give my children their best chance at a wonderful, healthy life.

Today I can say with confidence that my children have grown to be 100% better off than they would have been had I not gone through this metamorphosis. I am sharing the tools I used with other single moms. I want your family legacy to be healthy, happy, and whole.

Recommended Reading

Books that helped me during my single mom life:

1. *My Single Mom Life* — Angela Thomas

2. *Breathing Room* — Leanna Tankersley

3. *Uninvited* — Lysa Terkeurst

4. *The Land Between* — Jeff Manion

5. *The Gifts of Imperfection* — Brene Brown

6. *The Grief Recovery Handbook* — John W. James

7. *Codependent No More* — Melody Beattie

8. *The Purpose Driven Life* — Rick Warren

9. *Boundaries* — Henry Cloud

10. *Make Miracles in Forty Days* — Melody Beattie

11. *Jesus Calling* — Sarah Young